The Complete
Soup Maker
Recipe Book

Quick and Healthy Low-Carb Recipes For a Healthy Lifestyle

Copyright © 2020 by Jonathan C. Smith

ALL rights reserved

All rights for this book here presented belong exclusively to the author.
Usage or production of the next is forbidden and requires a clear
Consent of the author in
Case of expectations.

ISBN-9798418052698

TABLE OF CONTENTS

What is a soup maker?..5

How does a soup maker work?..5

Are there any soups my machine can't make? 6

Do you add all the ingredients at the same time? 6

What if I don't want my soup super smooth? 6

Health Benefits Of Soup 6

Delicious Soups to Try Right Now 9

    Soup maker broccoli and stilton soup..11

    Soup maker mushroom soup..12

    Soup maker butternut squash soup 13

    Soup maker carrot and coriander soup..14

    Soup maker tomato soup...15

    Soup maker vegetable soup...16

    Easy soup maker roast chicken soup...17

    Soup maker pea & ham soup 18

    Easy soup maker lentil soup 19

    Easy soup maker lentil soup 20

    Leek and Potato Soup in a Soup Maker 21

    Carrot and Turmeric..22

    Potato Cheddar Soup 23

    Red Pepper & Chilli Soup 24

    Apple and Parsnip Soup 25

    Weet Potato and Red Chili Soup 26

    Carrot and Coriander Soup 27

    Curried Parsnip Soup 28

    Spicy Bean Soup 28

    Chicken and Tarragon Soup 29

- Tasty Carrot and Ginger Soup 30
- Bacon and Lentil Soup 31
- Chicken Tikka Masala Soup 31
- Butter Bean and Lentil Soup 33
- Thai Red Curry Soup 33
- Cauliflower Cheese Soup 34
- Asparagus Soup 35
- Carrot and Sweet Potato Soup 35
- Carrot and Orange Soup 36
- Spiced Carrot Soup 36
- Broccoli and Cheese Soup 37
- Spicy Tomato Soup 38
- Moroccan Chickpea Soup 38
- Creamy Tomato & Rosemary Soup 39
- Minestrone Meatball Soup 40
- Beetroot Soup with Hummus Toast 41
- Zesty Sausage & Gnocchi Soup 42
- Chorizo & Bean Soup with Feta 42
- Prawn and Corn Soup 43
- French Onion Soup 44
- Mixed Pea and Ham Soup 45
- Gazpacho 46
- Curried Pumpkin Soup with Hummus 46
- Mixed Mushroom Soup with Haloumi 47
- Sweet Potato and Red Lentil Soup 48
- Pea and Broad Bean Soup with Prosciutto 49
- Roast Tomato and Basil Soup 50
- Butternut Squash, Chilli and Coconut Soup 51
- Quick and Easy Pea, Ham, and Mint Soup 52
- French Style Pistou 53
- Chinese Style Chicken and Sweetcorn Soup. 53
- Chicken and Mushroom Soup 54
- Winter Lamb and Lentil Broth 55
- Cauliflower Velouté with Chorizo Oil 56

Roasted Carrot and Coriander Soup 57
French Onion Soup with a Gruyère Crouton 58
Cream of Tomato Soup 59
Gazpacho with Rosemary Oil 61
Hot & Sour Soup 62
Pea & Coconut Soup 63
Roasted Jerusalem Artichoke Soup 64
Mulligatawny Soup 65
POTATO JALAPENO SOUP MAKER 66
Tomato & Basil Soup 67
Pumpkin soup 68
Curry soup with pumpkin and parsnip 68
TOMATO-CARROT SOUP 69
PEA SOUP 69
LETTUCE SOUP 70
SWEET POTATO-PEPPER SOUP 70
THOM KA KAI SOUP 71
Beetroot soup with healthy cream 72
Mixed vegetable soup for all seasons 73
Tomato-Red Bell Soup 74

Yes, soup is not reserved for children or elders. Soup has become trendy! Soup bars and franchises gain more and more popularity in urban areas as they are good alternatives to traditional fast food and snacks.

Soup is a star player disguised as an underrated appetizer. It can be a side or main dish, and the benefits of soup go beyond the bowl.

Sipping your soup in your styled cup while waiting in front of the metro station is more appealing than biting into your mayonnaise dripping sub sandwich or your fatty hamburger… not so sexy, is it?

What is a soup maker?

A soup maker is an all-in-one appliance that combines various blending functions to make your soup chunky or smooth (or however you like it), with a heating element or friction blades to cook a batch of soup in about 20 to 30 minutes. Soup makers typically resemble a blender or kettle.

How does a soup maker work?

Soup blenders take any fuss, and the standing-around-and-stirring time, out of soup making. There's no need for additional equipment, either – you don't need a stick blender or a liquidizer; this gadget does it all. You add the ingredients (only a slight peeling and chopping required) to the liquidizer and press a button.

It heats, stirs, and blends to make a soup that's table-ready within around 30 mins. It's great for busy schedules, people in shared accommodation when hob space is tight, or even makeshift kitchens or offices where there's no hob. You can press the button and walk away – similar to a slow cooker.

Are there any soups my machine can't make?

Tough herbs like bay leaves, rosemary stalks, or bouquet garnie are best avoided when using a soup maker. As the machine blends intermittently during cooking, tougher herbs will be broken up by the blades, and you won't be able to fish them out, later on, leaving your soup with tricky bits in.

Don't fill the soup maker past the max fill line. If you have too much stock, fill up to the bar, and once your soup is done, and you'd prefer a thinner consistency, add the hot stock, and mix it in.

Add dairy such as cheese, cream, crème fraîche, and yogurt after the soup has finished its cycle, so there's no chance of curdling.

Do you add all the ingredients at the same time?

If you want some texture in the soup, like ham, or chicken, it's best to stir this into the soup after it's cooked. Meat doesn't work very well, as it's broken up too much by the blades and loses its texture. It's the same for anything whole or larger chunks of ingredients you want to add to the soup.

What if I don't want my soup super smooth?

Most soup makers have a 'chunky' and a 'smooth' setting. This means you can still make chunky soups like minestrone, chicken and sweetcorn, or lentil soups; it just doesn't blend as much as the 'smooth' setting but still stirs, heats, and makes delicious soups in minutes.

Health Benefits Of Soup

It Helps Keep You Warm

When the temperatures outside reach freezing levels, nothing will warm you up like a bowl of soup. Unlike hot caffeinated beverages that leave you dehydrated, soup nourishes you from within and helps increase core body temperature. A bowl of your favorite soup will warm you from inside out on a cold, chilly night, keeping you toasty warm.

It Can Help Lose Weight

Research has found that people who regularly drink soup have lower dietary energy density and better diet quality. The high water and fiber content from vegetables added to soup keep you satiated in a healthy and hydrating way. Have a bowl of soup in the evening, and you will be unlikely to over-eat too many calories at dinner-time.

It Keeps You Satiated

Don't underestimate a good old bowl of soup. It makes for a hearty meal to provide high satiety with fewer calories than most other regular meals. Researchers from Oxford Brookes University, U.K., found that smooth soup induces greater fullness compared with the solid meal because of a combination of delayed gastric emptying. This can lead to feelings of gastric distension and rapid accessibility of nutrients, causing a more excellent glycemic response. In short, the soup will keep you feel for longer, keep your tummy happy and keep your blood sugar levels stable.

It's Good For Digestion

Unless you go for a soup laden with heavy cream, most recipes include fibrous vegetables, beans, lentils, and meats that ensure healthy digestion. Eating fiber-rich diet aids in smooth digestion and also increases insulin sensitivity.

Diet Quality

Measured against healthy eating standards, soup consumers have reduced total fat intake. They also have an increased protein intake, dietary fiber, and other nutrients.

While sodium intake needs to be monitored, people who eat soups are more likely to have an improved diet quality.

It's Power-Packed With Nutrients

For those who find it hard to eat 7-8 servings of vegetables a day, making a pot of soup to reheat and eat throughout the week is the solution. You can add a variety of vegetables to your soup, and it's also an excellent way to incorporate any leftovers and create a whole new dish. Plus, it's easy to add a variety of veggies into soups in a non-intrusive way, getting the pickiest of eaters to consume them. We can't think of a healthier meal the whole family can enjoy!

The Vitamins and Minerals Stay Intact

The slow cooking method used for soup ensures that it retains the vitamins and minerals of cooked vegetables since you also consume the broth. Whether you are making a soup with lentils, beans, or meat coupled with vegetables, you get a full array of nutrients in that delicious broth. Also, some nutrients like beta carotene from carrots and lycopene from tomatoes are better absorbed by the body when cooked rather than when eaten raw.

It Can Keep Aches and Pains At Bay

When making soup, don't discard the bones. If you slow-cook the whole carcass with bones, tendons, and ligaments to make your soup, you get a delicious bone broth that is high in gelatin, collagen, and glycine that have a natural anti-inflammatory effect. A bowl of bone broth can promote healthy bowel movements, improve gut motility, combat gut inflammation and naturally treat gut dysbiosis. It also helps boost immunity to keep stomach infections at bay.

It Is Naturally Healing

There is a reason the doctor tells you to have a warm bowl of pumpkin or chicken soup when you're fighting the flu. Studies have found that hot chicken soup is superior to other hot or cold liquids in managing fluids in upper respiratory tract infections. The nutrition-filled broth boosts immunity with essential vitamins and minerals and rehydrates your body. Also, it is easy to digest, which makes it perfect for when you have a sore throat or poor appetite. Plus, if you have a nasty cold, the hot vapors warm you up and help clear nasal passages.

Besides these benefits of soups, the thing we like most is that they're so versatile. You can play around with ratios and measurements to create a warming, delicious bowl of goodness with any ingredients at hand and use a variety of herbs and spices to try new flavors. As long as you keep a close eye on added salt, a bowl of soup will ALWAYS be a healthy option. Making soup is also inexpensive since you can use whatever you have lying around in the house.

What's better — soups are so easy to freeze and reheat. Make a large pot over the weekend, store it in airtight containers and freeze. You can reheat each portion of soup every weeknight or lunch the next day, and it'll only taste better each time!

Delicious Soups to Try Right Now

Now that you know all about the benefits of soup, it's time to try out these eight delicious recipes!

Chicken Soup

We love a bowl of gut-healing + immunity-boosting chicken soup on a cold chilly day. While there are great recipes to try, from a creamy smooth soup to a clear soup and even chunky chicken soup, we love the idea of a chicken soup that is soothing and nourishing for the gut. Add root vegetables that are easy to digest and promote a healthy inner ecosystem. Bump up the flavors with ginger and garlic that are anti-inflammatory and support immune function – perfect if you're fighting a cold or flu!

Pumpkin Soup

Pumpkin soup is an attractive option for anyone fighting indigestion and stomach infections and for those on a weight loss program. This soup is soothing, gentle, and easy to digest with soluble fibers that help keep you full. It's low in calories, high in energy, and can also help balance your electrolytes after a hard day.

Miso Soup

Looking for a bowl of soup that aids digestion, is full of healthy probiotics, and helps keep pains and aches at bay? Try miso soup! A bowl of traditional Japanese miso soup helps relieve fatigue, regulate digestive and intestinal functions, protect against gastric ulcers, boost heart health, prevent inflammation, and lower the risk of chronic ailments associated with poor lifestyle factors. In short — miso soup is a shining example of how food can work as medicine.

Tomato Soup

Tomatoes are rich in lycopene – a potent antioxidant that fights against oxidative stress caused by the free radicals to prevent inflammation and reduce the risk of chronic diseases. What's better, tomato soup is also filled with the goodness of Vitamin K and calcium that improve bone health, along with Vitamin A & C that improve cardiovascular health. We recommend a tomato basil soup that's high in flavor, easy to make, and freezes very well.

Lentil Soup

If you are vegetarian or vegan, lentil soup is a great way to get more proteins in your diet. What's better, lentil soup helps lower bad cholesterol because it contains high soluble fiber and is also good for heart health, digestive health, and stabilizing blood sugar levels. Add vegetables of your choice, and you will have a hearty meal that promotes weight loss and boosts energy levels.

Cabbage Soup

Who hasn't heard of the cabbage soup diet, right? But while eating nothing but cabbage soup for days is not the most appetizing idea, cabbage soup in itself offers a variety of health benefits when it's a part of a balanced diet. This soup is packed with fiber and vitamins B, C, and K. It can help you stay slim and detox the body of toxins. It's also great for gastrointestinal health. Add various herbs and spices to boost flavors, and cook your cabbage in chicken or beef broth for added taste.

Spinach Soup

Rich in antioxidants and packed with nutrients, a bowl of green spinach soup is a great way to warm your body inside out. It's a natural anti-inflammatory, boosts cognitive function and memory, and is excellent for bone health. Add ginger and garlic to your spinach soup to boost its anti-inflammatory action and give it some extra heat.

Asparagus Soup

If you suffer from insulin resistance or diabetes, try asparagus soup. A great source of fiber, folate, vitamins A, C, E, and K, as well as chromium, a bowl of asparagus soup can enhance insulin's ability to transport glucose from the bloodstream into cells. Add chopped asparagus with onion and garlic to a pot with low-sodium chicken broth and simmer away. Throw in a handful of fresh herbs, such as thyme, dill, or basil for new flavors, along with two tablespoons of grated Parmigiano-Reggiano and a dash of freshly squeezed lemon juice for a nourishing, delectable bowl of asparagus soup for the soul.

Soup maker broccoli and stilton soup

Prep Time 5 minutes Cook Time 30 minutes Serves 4

Ingredients

- 1 onion, finely chopped
- 1 celery stick, sliced
- 1 leek, sliced

- 1 medium potato, diced
- 750ml low salt or homemade chicken or vegetable stock
- 1 head broccoli, roughly chopped
- 140g stilton, or other blue cheese, crumbled

Method

1. Put all the ingredients into the soup maker, except the stilton, and press the 'smooth soup' function. Make sure you don't fill the soup maker above the max fill line.
2. Once the cycle is complete, season and stir in most of the stilton, blend briefly again until the cheese has melted into the soup—season with black pepper and top with the reserved cheese to serve.

Nutrition Per Serving: Kcal 275, Fat 14g, Saturates 8g, Carbs 17g, Sugars 7g, Fibre 8g, Protein 16g, Salt 1.2g

Soup maker mushroom soup

Prep Time 5 minutes Cook Time 20 minutes Serves 4

Ingredients

- 2 medium onions, roughly chopped
- 1 garlic clove, crushed
- 500g mushrooms, finely chopped (chestnut or button mushrooms work well)
- 750ml chicken stock

- 4 tbsp single cream, plus more to serve
- small handful flat-leaf parsley, roughly chopped, to serve (optional)

Method

1. Put the onions, garlic, mushrooms, and stock into the soup maker, and press the 'smooth soup' function. Make sure you don't fill the soup maker above the max fill line.
2. Once the cycle is complete, season well, and stir in the cream. Blend briefly again until the soup is creamy, then serve in bowls topped with the parsley and more cream if you like.

Nutrition Per Serving: fat 4g, Saturates 2g, Carbs 6g, Sugars 5g, Fibre 3g, Protein 9g, Salt 1.08g

Soup maker butternut squash soup

Prep Time 5 minutes Cook Time 30 minutes Serves 4

Make a batch of this warming butternut squash soup in a soup maker for a leisurely lunch or supper. The chilli gives it a nice kick

Ingredients

- ½ butternut squash (about 500g), peeled and chopped into 4cm cubes
- ½ tbsp olive oil

- 1 onion, diced
- 1 small garlic clove, thinly sliced
- 1 mild red chilli, deseeded and finely chopped
- 400ml vegetable stock
- 2 tbsp crème fraîche, plus more to serve

Method

1. Heat the oven to 200C/180C fan/gas 6. Toss the butternut squash in a roasting tin with olive oil. Season and roast for 30 mins, turning once during cooking, until golden and soft.
2. Put the roast squash into the soup maker, along with the onion, garlic, most of the chilli, and all the stock. Make sure you don't fill the soup maker above the max fill line. Season well. Press the 'smooth soup' function.
3. Season well once the cycle is complete and add the crème fraîche. Blend briefly once again until the soup is creamy. Add a little extra stock or boiling water if you prefer a thinner soup, and serve in bowls with a swirl of crème fraîche and the reserved chopped chilli.

Nutrition Per Serving: Kcal 272, Fat 15g, Saturates 9g, Carbs 28g, Sugars 7g, Fibre 3g, Protein 5g, Salt 0.53g

Soup maker carrot and coriander soup

Prep Time 5 minutes Cook Time 30 minutes Serves 4

Blend this comforting and colorful carrot and coriander soup in a soup maker. Serve straight away with crusty bread or freeze it

Ingredients

- 1 small onion, chopped

- ½ tsp ground coriander
- 1 small potato, peeled and chopped
- 400g carrots, peeled and chopped
- 600ml vegetable or chicken stock
- ½ small bunch of coriander

Method

1. Put all the ingredients into the soup maker, except the coriander, and press the 'smooth soup' function. Make sure you don't fill the soup maker above the max fill line.
2. Once the cycle is complete, season and add the coriander and blend once again until the coriander is mixed well and served.

Nutrition Per Serving: kcal 133, fat 2g, Saturates 1g, Carbs 17g, Sugars 11g, Fibre 7g, Protein 9g, Salt 1.83g

Soup maker tomato soup

Make this tasty tomato soup in a soup maker for delicious results with minimal effort. It's low in calories and fat and delivers two of your 5-a-day

Prep Time 5 minutes Cook Time 30 minutes Serves 4

Ingredients

- 500g ripe tomatoes, off the vine and quartered or halved
- 1 small onion, chopped

- ½ small carrot, chopped
- ½ celery stick, chopped
- 1 tsp tomato purée
- pinch of sugar
- 450ml vegetable stock

Method

1. Put all the ingredients into the soup maker and press the 'smooth soup' function. Make sure you don't fill the soup maker above the max fill line.
2. Once the cycle is complete, season well, check the soup for sweetness. Add a little more sugar, salt, or tomato puree for depth of color, if you like.

Nutrition: Per serving Kcal 85, Fat 1g, Saturates 0g, Carbs 14g, Sugars 13g, Fibre 5g, Protein 3g, Salt 0.62g

Soup maker vegetable soup

Whizz up this versatile vegetable soup in a soup maker using your favourite vegetables. Serve with a dollop of crème fraîche and some herbs

Prep Time 5 minutes Cook Time 30 minutes Serves 2

Ingredients

- 200g vegetables, such as onions, celery and carrots, chopped
- 300g potato, peeled and chopped
- 700ml vegetable stock

- crème fraîche and fresh herbs, to serve

Method

1. Put the vegetables, potatoes, and stock into a soup blender, and press the 'smooth soup' function. Make sure you don't fill the soup maker above the max fill line.
2. Once the cycle is complete, season and pour into bowls with a dollop of crème fraîche and some herbs.

Nutrition Per Serving: kcal 166, fat 1g, Saturates 0g, Carbs 32g, Sugars 9g, Fibre 7g, Protein 4g, Salt 0.95g

Easy soup maker roast chicken soup

Make a comforting roast chicken soup with the help of a soup maker. It's excellent using leftover chicken from a Sunday roast, and it's easy to freeze

Prep Time 5 minutes Cook Time 30 minutes Serves 2

Ingredients

- 1 onion, chopped
- 1 large carrot, chopped
- ½ tbsp thyme leaves, roughly chopped
- 700ml chicken stock
- 100g frozen peas

- 150g leftover roast chicken, shredded and skin removed
- 1½ tbsp Greek yogurt
- ½ small garlic clove, crushed
- squeeze lemon juice

Method

1. Put the onion, carrot, thyme, stock, and peas into a soup maker, and press the 'chunky soup' function. Make sure you don't fill the soup maker above the max fill line.
2. Once the cycle is complete, stir in the shredded roast chicken, and leave to warm through while mixing the yogurt, garlic and lemon juice. Season the soup, and pour into bowls. Stir in some of the yogurt and serve.

Nutrition Per Serving: Kcal 155, Fat 5g, Saturates 2g, Carbs 8g, Sugars 6g, Fibre 4g, Protein 17g, Salt 1.11g,

Soup maker pea & ham soup

Make a traditional pea and ham soup using a soup maker. It's perfect for a light lunch or supper served with bread and delivers two of your 5-a-day

Prep Time 5 minutes Cook Time 30 minutes Serves 4

Ingredients

- 1 onion, chopped
- 1 medium potato, peeled and diced
- 1litre ham or pork stock

- 500g frozen petit pois
- 300g thickly sliced ham, trimmed of any fat and diced

Method

1. Put the onion, potatoes, stock and peas into a soup blender, and press the 'smooth soup' function. Make sure you don't fill the soup maker above the max fill line.
2. Once the cycle is complete, season and stir in the ham before serving.

Nutrition Per Serving: Kcal 260, Fat 6g, Saturates 2g, Carbs 24g, Sugars 10g, Fibre 8g, Protein 24g, Salt 3.98g

Easy soup maker lentil soup

Use a soup maker to make this easy lentil soup with leek and carrot for lunch or supper. It's filling and nutritious, plus low in calories and fat

Prep Time 5 minutes Cook Time 30 minutes Serves 4

Ingredients

- 750ml vegetable or ham stock
- 75g red lentils
- 3 carrots, finely chopped
- 1 medium leek, sliced (150g)
- small handful chopped parsley, to serve

Method

1. Put the stock, lentils, carrots and leek into a soup maker, and press the 'chunky soup' function. Make sure you don't fill it above the max fill line. The soup will look a little foamy to start, but don't worry – it will disappear once cooked.
2. Once the cycle is complete, check the tender lentils and season well. Scatter over the parsley to serve.

Nutrition Per Serving: Kcal 103, Fat 1g, Saturates 0g, Carbs 15g, Sugars 5g, Fibre 5g, Protein 6g, Salt 0.15g,

Easy soup maker lentil soup

Use a soup maker to make this easy lentil soup with leek and carrot for lunch or supper. It's filling and nutritious, plus low in calories and fat

Prep Time 5 minutes Cook Time 30 minutes Serves 4

Ingredients

- 750ml vegetable or ham stock
- 75g red lentils
- 3 carrots, finely chopped
- 1 medium leek, sliced (150g)
- small handful chopped parsley, to serve

Method

1. Put the stock, lentils, carrots and leek into a soup maker, and press the 'chunky soup' function. Make sure you don't fill it above the max fill line. The soup will look a little foamy to start, but don't worry – it will disappear once cooked.
2. Once the cycle is complete, check the tender lentils and season well. Scatter over the parsley to serve.

Nutrition Per Serving: kcal 103, fat 1g, Saturates 0g, Carbs 15g, Sugars 5g, Fibre 5g, Protein 6g, Salt 0.15g

Leek and Potato Soup in a Soup Maker

Prep Time 5 minutes Cook Time 20 minutes Serves 4

Ingredients

- 2 medium leeks, sliced
- 300g potato, peeled and diced
- 1 onion, chopped
- 2 cloves garlic, peeled and crushed
- 1-litre vegetable stock

Method

1. Prepare the ingredients by peeling the onion and chopping it up, trimming the roots and tops of the leeks and finely slicing, peeling the garlic cloves and crushing and peeling and dicing the potatoes.
2. Optional: add 1 tbsp. Olive oil to either your soup maker (if it has a sauté function) or a saucepan. Gently sauté the onions for 2 minutes, stirring frequently. Add the leeks and garlic and sauté for a further 2 to 3 minutes until they start to soften.
3. Switch off the sauté function/transfer ingredients to your soup maker. Add the potatoes to the soup maker.
4. Add approximately 1 litre of vegetable stock (make sure you stay within the minimum and maximum guidelines on your soup maker)
5. Stir the ingredients around with a wooden spoon. Set the soup maker off on a smooth setting.
6. Season according to taste.

Carrot and Turmeric

Prep Time 10 minutes Cook Time 20 minutes Serves 4

Ingredients

- 400 g Carrots chopped.
- 150 g Leek chopped.
- 200 g Potatoes chopped.
- Tablespoon Rapeseed oil.
- Teaspoon Salt.
- Teaspoon Ground Pepper.
- Tablespoon Turmeric Powder.
- 1 Chicken Stock Cube.
- 450 ml Chicken Stock - I used Tesco.
- Water to maximum fill level for 1600ml soup.
- 200 ml Heavy Cream Double Cream.

Method

1. Add your rapeseed oil to the pan or the soupmaker and saute with the leek until the leek is soft.
2. Add the remaining ingredients, stirring well. The soup looks somewhat unappetising at this point. Don't let it put you off. See the thumbnail image above.
3. Choose your cooking setting. I chose smooth for my version, as I wanted a creamy, luxurious soup rather than a meal in a bowl type soup.
4. When fully cooked, pour in the cream slowly, then stir before eating. If you plan to freeze, do so before adding dairy, as soup with cream does not defrost well.

Potato Cheddar Soup

Prep Time 10 minutes Cook Time 30 minutes Serves 2

Ingredients

- 30 g (1 tbsp) butter
- 1 small onion
- 1 teaspoon minced garlic
- 1 teaspoon Italian herbs
- ½ teaspoon thyme
- 250 g (1 cup) potatoes
- 1 medium carrot
- 2 celery sticks
- 75 g (¾ cup) mature Cheddar
- 500 ml (2 ½ cups) vegetable stock
- 50 ml (¼ cup) double (heavy) cream
- 2 Italian sausages, cases removed
- Salt and pepper

Method

1. Cut all vegetables in large chunks and set them aside.
2. Add the butter, onion, garlic and herbs to the soup maker and cook on "saute" or similar setting depending on your model for 5 minutes.
3. Add all the vegetables, Cheddar, and stock, and use the "smooth" or "creamy" setting on your soup maker.
4. When there are 2-3 minutes left, add the double cream.
5. In the meantime, fry the Italian sausage in a small pan until golden and crisp.
6. When the soup maker is done, season with salt and pepper, pour the soup into bowls and sprinkle the sausage on top.
7. Serve immediately with crusty bread or another side of choice.

Nutrition Per serving: Calories: 375Total Fat: 27gSaturated Fat: 14gTrans Fat: 1g

Red Pepper & Chilli Soup

Red pepper and chilli soup is a deliciously warming recipe with a spicy kick from the fresh chilli. It's quick and easy to make in a soup maker!

Prep Time 5 minutes Cook Time 10 minutes Serves 2

Ingredients

- 1 onion, chopped
- 2 red peppers, chopped
- 2 garlic cloves, crushed
- 1 potato, medium (approx 200g), chopped
- 1 red chilli, sliced (deseed for a milder taste)
- 750 ml chicken or vegetable stock (using 1 stock cube or pot)

Method

1. Add all the ingredients to the soup maker.
2. Add the stockpot or cube and top up hot water to the M.A.X. line.
3. Stir ingredients around and set off on the smooth program.
4. Add any additional seasoning and optionally add croutons.

Apple and Parsnip Soup

Prep Time 10 minutes Cook Time 20 minutes Serves 4

Ingredients

- 1 tbsp olive oil
- 2 Granny Smith apples
- 4 parsnips
- 1 tsp ground cinnamon
- 1 onion
- 1-litre vegetable stock

Method

1. Peel and chop the apples, parsnips and onion.
2. Heat the oil and saute the onion (optional)
3. Add remaining ingredients. If the stock does not reach the MIN level, you may need to top up with a little hot water. Alternatively, for a thicker soup, add more parsnips and apples.
4. Set off on smooth.

Weet Potato and Red Chili Soup

Prep Time 10 minutes Cook Time 15 minutes Serves 2

Ingredients

- 1 tbsp olive oil
- 800 g sweet potatoes, peeled and chopped
- 1 onion, peeled and chopped
- 3 cloves garlic, crushed
- 1 (or 2!) red chillies, sliced (deseed for a milder taste)
- 800 ml vegetable stock

Method

1. Optional: Saute onions and garlic in olive oil for up to 5 minutes.
2. Add all ingredients to the soup maker. Make sure you remain within the MIN and M.A.X. soup maker levels. Top up with more stock/hot water if required.
3. Set soup maker off on to smooth.

Carrot and Coriander Soup

Prep Time 5 minutes Cook Time 15 minutes Serves 4

Ingredients

- 1 tbsp olive oil
- 800 g carrots, roughly chopped
- 1 onion, chopped
- 1 tsp ground coriander
- 1-litre vegetable stock
- fresh coriander, a large handful

Method

1. Optional: Saute chopped onions in olive oil
2. Add remaining ingredients apart from fresh coriander
3. Set off on smooth
4. At the end of the cycle, remove the Lid and add fresh coriander. Stir into soup
5. Optional: Blend manually to puree the coriander leaves for a completely smooth soup.
6. Season if required

Amount Per Serving: calories: 111g

Curried Parsnip Soup

Prep Time 5 minutes Cook Time 20 minutes Serves 4

Ingredients

- 1 onion, peeled and chopped
- 5 parsnips, medium and chopped
- 1 carrot, medium and chopped
- 2 tsp curry powder
- 1-litre vegetable stock (adjust according to soup maker levels)
- Pinch crushed red chillies (Optional)

Method

1. Optional: sauté onion in butter or oil. Add onion and sauté for a few minutes.
2. Add all remaining ingredients. Check minimum required level is reached - add more stock if needed.
3. Set off on smooth.
4. You can optionally stir in some cream at the end of the cycle.
5. Sprinkle with crushed red chillies (optional)

Spicy Bean Soup

Spicy bean soup is quick to make in a soup maker - make it on chunky or smooth - it tastes perfect with a large chunk of crusty bread dipped in!

Prep Time 5 minutes Cook Time 30 minutes Serves 4

Ingredients

- 1 onion, chopped
- 2 cloves garlic, crushed
- 1 x tin 400g mixed beans
- 1 x tin 400g chopped tomatoes or passata
- 2 tsp chilli powder
- 1/2 tsp ground cumin
- 1/2 tsp ground coriander
- 1 vegetable stock cube/pot

Method

1. Optionally saute the onion and garlic.
2. Add all the ingredients to the soup maker.
3. Add hot water up to the line and stir to combine.
4. Put the Lid on and select the smooth or chunky setting, depending on your preferences.
5. You can partially blend the soup to alter consistency at the end of the soup-making cycle. Manually combine or pulse for a few seconds.
6. Serve with grated cheese, tortilla crisps and a swirl of cream if desired.

Chicken and Tarragon Soup

Prep Time 5 minutes Cook Time 20 minutes Serves 4

Ingredients

- 150 g cooked chicken, shredded/chopped
- 1 vegetable stock cube
- 2 tbsp fresh tarragon, finely chopped
- 150 ml double cream
- 1 onion, peeled and chopped
- 2 cloves garlic, crushed
- 1 tbsp olive oil

Method

1. If the cooked chicken isn't already sliced up, chop it into smaller pieces.
2. Gently heat the oil and sauté your chopped onions. If you have one with this function, this can be done in your soup maker. If not, you can do this in a

separate saucepan. (Sautéeing is optional - you can throw the onions in as they are if you prefer).
3. Switch the sauté function off/transfer onions to the saucepan.
4. Add chicken, chopped tarragon, crushed garlic and vegetable stock cube.
5. Fill the soup maker up to at least the minimum line with hot water (depending on how thin/thick you want it).
6. Stir to mix all ingredients.
7. Set soup maker off to smooth.
8. Once the soup maker is finished, stir in the double cream.
9. Serve with some sprinkled tarragon (optional).

Tasty Carrot and Ginger Soup

Prep Time 5 minutes Cook Time 20 minutes Serves 4

Ingredients

- 2-3 tbsp fresh root ginger*, grated
- 1 onion, chopped
- 600g carrots, peeled, chopped
- 2 garlic cloves, crushed
- 750ml vegetable stock (approx)
- Seasoning of your choice (optional)

Method

1. Optional: sauté the onion, garlic and ginger.
2. Add the remaining ingredients taking care not to go over the M.A.X. soup level.
3. Place the Lid on the soup maker and select the smooth setting.
4. Season according to taste.

Bacon and Lentil Soup

Prep Time 5 minutes Cook Time 20 minutes Serves 4

Ingredients

- 1 tbsp olive oil
- 4 rashers bacon, fat removed, chopped
- 1 medium onion, chopped
- 200 g split red lentils, rinsed
- 1 medium potato, chopped
- 1 small carrot, chopped
- 1-litre chicken stock

Method

1. If your soup maker has a sauté function, heat the oil and cook the onions and bacon. If your soup maker doesn't have to sauté, you can do this in a pan on the hob.
2. Add all the remaining ingredients and give it a good stir to make sure nothing is stuck to the bottom.
3. Set the soup maker off on smooth.

Chicken Tikka Masala Soup

Prep Time 10 minutes Cook Time 25 minutes Serves 4

Ingredients

- 3-4 chicken breasts, cooked, shredded/diced
- 1 tbsp oil
- 1 onion, sliced
- 3 cloves garlic, crushed
- 4 tbsp chicken tikka powder

- 1 tsp ground ginger
- 300 g passata
- 800 ml chicken stock
- 150 ml double or single cream, or swap with natural yoghurt
- fresh coriander, optional garnish

Method

1. If you are not using leftover cooked chicken, you will need to precook the chicken now (oven, fry or however you usually cook chicken).
2. If you have a sauté function on your soup maker, heat the oil and cook the onions for a couple of minutes. If you don't have a sauté function, it is worth doing this step in a pan on the hob to infuse the onion spices.
3. Add the crushed garlic and sauté for a further minute.
4. Add the chicken tikka spices and ground ginger and sauté for another minute. You might find that some of the herbs stick to the base of the soup maker if they do pour in a little of the hot stock to deglaze (use a wooden spoon to scrape off any stuck spices). This will also create a paste-like liquid.
5. Switch off the sauté function and add the cooked chicken, passata and stock. Ensure that you are between your soup maker's MIN and M.A.X. lines.
6. Stir the ingredients so that they are well mixed.
7. Place the Lid on the soup maker and set it off in the chunky setting.
8. If you add rice to your soup, you can cook it now.
9. Once the soup has finished, lift the Lid off and stir in the cream. You can also go in your cooked rice if you have that.
10. Optionally garnish with fresh coriander.

Butter Bean and Lentil Soup

Prep Time 5 minutes Cook Time 20 minutes Serves 4

Ingredients

- 1 tbsp olive oil/butter, or your usual oil
- 1 onion, chopped
- 1 clove garlic, crushed
- 400 g tin butter beans
- 120 g red split lentils, washed
- 300 g passata
- 1 tsp ground coriander
- 800 ml vegetable stock
- 1/2 tsp crushed red chillies (optional)

Method

1. Optional: Sauté onion & garlic in soup maker in some oil or butter.
2. Switch off sauté and add all remaining ingredients (apart from crushed red chillies)
3. Stir contents well.
4. Set off on smooth.
5. Optional: sprinkle crushed chillies on top.

Thai Red Curry Soup

Prep Time 10 minutes Cook Time 30 minutes Serves 4

Ingredients

- 1 tbsp oil
- 300g chicken, approx. two breasts (cooked if using Morphy Richards, or raw if using Ninja, see notes below)
- 2 cloves garlic, crushed
- 1 tbsp fresh ginger, grated/1tsp ground ginger
- 4-5 tbsp Thai Red Curry Paste
- 1 lemongrass stalk

- 2 kaffir lime leaves
- 1 red chilli, chopped
- 4 spring onions, chopped
- 200ml coconut milk
- 700ml chicken stock
- 50g dry egg noodles

Method

1. Optional: saute garlic & ginger for 1 min
2. Switch off sauté and add red curry paste, stir well to mix in with garlic & ginger.
3. Add remaining ingredients and stir well to make sure nothing is stuck to the base of the soup maker.
4. Set off on chunky.
5. Stir in cooked noodles/rice if you wish.
6. Optionally garnish with fresh coriander.

Cauliflower Cheese Soup

Prep Time 5 minutes Cook Time 20 minutes Serves 4

Ingredients

- 400g to 450g cauliflower florets, approx
- 1 small onion, chopped
- 2 cloves garlic, sliced
- 1 small potato, scrubbed or peeled and chopped
- 150 g cheddar cheese, grated
- 950 ml vegetable stock

Method

1. Try to break the cauliflower florets up as small as you can, or you might struggle to fit everything below the M.A.X. line.
2. Add all ingredients apart from the cheese.
3. Give everything a good stir to make sure no ingredients are stuck to the bottom or side of the soup maker.
4. Set off on smooth.

5. When the cycle has finished, lift the Lid off and stir in the grated cheddar cheese until melted.

Asparagus Soup

Prep Time 5 minutes Cook Time 20 minutes Serves 4

Ingredients

- 400g asparagus, chopped into small pieces
- 1 medium onion, chopped
- 1 clove garlic, crushed
- 1 medium potato, diced
- 2 sticks celery, finely sliced
- 850ml vegetable stock

Method

1. Add all the ingredients to your soup maker and mix.
2. Set off on smooth.

Carrot and Sweet Potato Soup

Prep Time 10 minutes Cook Time 20 minutes Serves 4

Ingredients

- 500g sweet potatoes, chopped
- 300g carrots, chopped
- 1 onion, chopped
- 1 clove garlic, sliced
- 900ml vegetable stock
- Seasoning according to taste

Method

- Optional: Saute the onions and garlic.
- Add all the ingredients to the soup maker.
- Add the vegetable stock up to between the max lines.

- Set off on smooth.

Carrot and Orange Soup

Prep Time 5 minutes Cook Time 25 minutes Serves 4

Ingredients

- 1 onion, chopped
- 1 clove garlic, crushed
- 500g carrots* chopped
- 1 medium potato (approx. 150g), chopped
- Optional spices (try cumin, chilli or mixed spices)
- 300ml fresh orange juice
- Vegetable stock (to the M.A.X. line for soup makers)
- Seasoning to taste

Method

1. Optionally sauté the onion and garlic in your soup maker.
2. Add the remaining ingredients to the soup maker jug. (I added 1 tsp of mixed spices)
3. Add a stockpot/cube and top up the M.A.X. line with hot water.
4. Set off on smooth.
5. Season according to taste.
6. Optionally add in some crème fraiche.

Spiced Carrot Soup

Prep Time 5 minutes Cook Time 25 minutes Serves 4

Ingredients

- 1 onion, chopped
- 1 clove garlic, crushed
- 500g carrots, chopped
- 1 medium potato (optional)
- 2tsp curry powder (add more if you prefer extra spice)
- Vegetable or chicken stock up to the line

Method

1. Add all the ingredients to the soup maker jug.
2. Top up with hot water, up to the M.A.X. line.
3. Set off on smooth.

Broccoli and Cheese Soup

Prep Time 5 minutes Cook Time 25 minutes Serves 4

Ingredients

- 200g fresh broccoli florets
- 1 medium potato
- 1 onion, sliced
- 1 clove garlic, crushed
- 800ml chicken/vegetable stock (approx.)
- 100g cheddar cheese, grated

Method

1. Apart from the cheese, add all the ingredients to the soup maker jug, making sure you don't go over the M.A.X. line of your soup maker.
2. Set off on smooth.
3. Once the soup maker cycle has finished, pour the finished soup into a bowl(s).
4. Stir some grated cheese into each bowl; your added amount will depend on how cheesy you like it!
5. Season to taste if required.

Spicy Tomato Soup

Prep Time 5 minutes Cook Time 25 minutes Serves 4

Ingredients

- 1 onion, peeled and chopped
- 2 cloves garlic, peeled and crushed
- 5 fresh tomatoes, quartered
- 1 red chilli, sliced (remove seeds for milder heat)
- 1tsp fresh ginger (grated)
- 1/2 tsp ground cumin
- Vegetable stock (up to max line)

Method

1. If your soup maker has a saute function, gently heat the onion, garlic and ginger in a bit of oil or butter.
2. Add the remaining ingredients and give everything a good stir round.
3. Set off on smooth.
4. Optionally top with fresh herbs, croutons, a swirl of cream, or grated cheese.

Moroccan Chickpea Soup

Prep Time 5 minutes Cook Time 25 minutes Serves 4

Ingredients

- 1 onion, chopped

- 2 garlic cloves, crushed
- 1 medium carrot, chopped
- 1 celery stalk, chopped
- 1 tin chickpeas (400g) (rinsed and drained)
- 1 tin chopped tomatoes (400g)
- 1/2 tsp each ground cumin, cinnamon, paprika and Cayenne pepper
- 800ml vegetable stock (or up to the M.A.X. line)
- Fresh mint leaves, chopped (optional for garnish)

Method

1. Optional Step: Heat a little oil in your soup maker (if it has a saute function) and add the onion, garlic and celery, saute for 5 minutes or the program length on your soup maker.
2. Add the remaining ingredients to your soup maker, taking care not to go over the M.A.X. line.
3. Give everything a good stir.
4. Put the Lid on and set off on the smooth setting.
5. Garnish with chopped mint leaves (optional).

Creamy Tomato & Rosemary Soup

Prep Time 5 minutes Cook Time 25 minutes Serves 4

Ingredients

- 1 stick celery, chopped
- 75g cooked smoked bacon, finely chopped
- 1 lion shallot, chopped
- 1 medium carrot, chopped
- 400g sweet ripe tomatoes on the vine, roughly chopped
- 1 x 390g carton thickly chopped tomatoes
- 2 cloves garlic, chopped
- 30ml white wine
- 400ml good vegetable stock
- 1 tbsp fresh chopped rosemary
- 1 tbsp fresh chopped thyme
- 1 tsp maple syrup

- salt and freshly ground black pepper
- 1 tbsp fresh chopped parsley
- 125ml double cream
- A swirl of cream and sprigs of rosemary to garnish

Method

1. Place the celery, bacon, shallot, carrot, tomatoes, garlic, wine, stock, rosemary, thyme and maple syrup in the Soup-Maker. Season. Choose the Creamed Soup setting.
2. Uncover and stir in parsley and cream—season to taste.
3. Meanwhile, warm four soup bowls. Divide the soup between the bowls and top each with a swirl of cream and fresh rosemary leaves. Season and serve.
4. Suitable for freezing.

Minestrone Meatball Soup

Prep Time 5 minutes Cook Time 25 minutes Serves 4

Ingredients

- 100g brown onion, finely chopped
- 100g zucchini, diced
- 100g carrot, diced
- 80g green beans, cut into 2cm pieces
- 1 clove garlic, crushed
- 400g can diced tomato
- 2 2/3 cups hot beef stock
- 1 cup passata
- 1 cup cooked risoni or macaroni
- 12 pre-made lamb or beef meatballs
- To Serve - Basil pesto and freshly
- grated parmesan cheese

Method

1. Place the onion, zucchini, carrot, beans, garlic, canned tomato, passata, hot stock, and pasta into the soup mug—season with salt.
2. Place the Lid on and select the Chunky setting, then press start.

3. Meanwhile, heat the Morphy Richards Multifunction Pot using the griddle pan to medium heat. Add meatballs; cook for around 5 minutes or until browned and cooked.
4. Serve soup in bowls add meatballs. Top with pesto and parmesan.

Beetroot Soup with Hummus Toast

Prep Time 5 minutes Cook Time 25 minutes Serves 4

Ingredients:

- 200g beetroot, peeled, cubed
- 100g potato, cubed
- 100g carrot, cubed
- 100g parsnip, cubed
- 80g shredded cabbage
- 1 celery stick, finely chopped
- 60g green beans, cut into 2cm pieces
- 1 small brown onion, finely chopped
- 3 cups hot vegetable stock
- 1 clove garlic, crushed
- Sliced rye sourdough baguette, toasted
- Hummus
- To Serve - chopped parsley and
- smoked paprika

Method

1. Place the vegetables, stock and garlic into the Soup Maker Jug. Season with salt.
2. Place the Lid on and select the Chunky setting, then press start.
3. Toast bread and spread with hummus and a sprinkle of smoked paprika.
4. Serve soup in bowls and garnish with parsley. Serve with toast.

Zesty Sausage & Gnocchi Soup

Prep Time 5 minutes Cook Time 25 minutes Serves 4

Ingredients

- 150g red capsicum, finely chopped
- 2 celery sticks, finely chopped
- 1 small onion, finely chopped
- 2 cloves garlic, crushed
- 1 teaspoon ground fennel
- 2 3/4 cups hot beef stock
- 2 cups passata
- 2 tablespoons olive oil
- 500g packet baby potato gnocchi
- 2 pork sausages
- To serve - Shaved parmesan, rosemary,
- grated lemon zest and pepper

Method

1. Place the capsicum, celery, onion, garlic, ground fennel, beef stock and pasta into the Soup Maker Jug. Season with salt.
2. Place the Lid on and select the Chunky setting, then press start.
3. Meanwhile, heat oil in a large frying pan over medium-high heat. Add gnocchi; cook, stirring, for 3 minutes or until golden and tender. Transfer to a bowl.
4. Squeeze sausage meat from casings. Roll into small balls. Add to pan; cook, stirring, for 3 minutes or until browned and cooked.
5. Pour soup into serving bowls. Top with gnocchi and sausage. Sprinkle with parmesan, rosemary, zest and pepper to serve.

Chorizo & Bean Soup with Feta

Prep Time 5 minutes Cook Time 25 minutes Serves 4

Ingredients

- 100g carrot, cubed
- 100g swede, cubed
- 1 small brown onion, finely chopped

- 1 celery stick, finely chopped
- 80g frozen peas, thawed
- 2 x 400g cans diced tomatoes
- 2 cups hot chicken stock
- 2 tablespoons tomato paste
- 2 chorizo sausages, sliced
- 400g can use four bean mix, drained and rinsed
- To Serve - Crumbled feta and oregano

Method

1. Place the carrot, swede, onion, celery, canned tomato, chicken stock and tomato paste into the Soup Maker Jug. Season with salt.
2. Place the Lid on and select the Chunky setting, then press start.
3. Meanwhile, heat a small frying pan over medium-high heat. Add chorizo; cook for 1 minute on each side or until browned.
4. Stir beans and peas into soup, return Lid and set to keep warm for 5 minutes to heat through beans and peas.
5. Serve soup into bowls and top with feta, chorizo and oregano to serve.

Prawn and Corn Soup

Prep Time 5 minutes Cook Time 25 minutes Serves 4

Ingredients:

- 400g can corn kernels, drained and rinsed
- 310g can creamed corn
- 100g pumpkin, cubed
- 1 small brown onion, finely chopped
- 1 clove garlic, crushed
- 1 cup white wine

- 2 cups hot vegetable stock
- 40g garlic butter
- 12 medium uncooked prawns,
- peeled, deveined
- To Serve - Croutons and dill sprigs

Method

1. Place the corn kernels, creamed corn, pumpkin, onion, garlic, wine and stock into the Soup Maker Jug. Season with salt.
2. Place the Lid on and select the Smooth setting, then press start.
3. Meanwhile, heat butter in a frying pan over medium heat. Add prawns; cook for 2 minutes on each side or until curled and browned.
4. Press and hold the Smoothie/Blend Button when the soup is finished. Repeat as necessary until desired consistency is achieved.
5. Pour soup into serving bowls. Top with prawns, croutons and dill.

French Onion Soup

Prep Time 5 minutes Cook Time 25 minutes Serves 4

Ingredients:

- 3 large onions, sliced
- 100g carrot, finely chopped
- 2 cloves garlic, crushed
- 3 cups hot vegetable stock
- 1 cup white wine
- ¼ teaspoon dried thyme
- ½ baguette, sliced

- 1 cup grated cheese
- Thyme sprigs, to serve

Method

1. Place the onion, garlic, stock, wine and dried thyme into the Soup Maker Jug. Season with salt.
2. Place the Lid on and select the Chunky setting, then press start.
3. Meanwhile, preheat an oven grill—place bread on an oven tray and top with cheese. Place under the grill and cook for 2 minutes or until cheese melts.
4. Remove ½ cup of sliced onion and reserve. Place the Lid on and press and hold the Smoothie/Blend Button. Repeat as necessary until desired consistency is achieved.
5. Pour soup into bowls. Top with cheese croutons, reserved sliced onion and thyme sprigs to serve.

Mixed Pea and Ham Soup

Prep Time 5 minutes Cook Time 25 minutes Serves 4

Ingredients:

- 1 cup dried green split peas, cooked
- 1 1/3 cups frozen peas
- 100g potato, finely chopped
- 1 small onion, finely chopped
- 2 cloves garlic, crushed
- 3 1/4 cups hot vegetable stock
- Blanched edamame beans, chopped
- leg ham and pine nuts, to serve

Method

1. Place the cooked split peas, frozen peas, potato, onion, garlic and stock into the Soup Maker Jug. Season with salt.
2. Place the Lid on and select the Chunky setting, then press start.
3. When cooked through, press and hold the Smoothie/Blend Button, repeat as necessary until desired consistency is achieved.
4. Pour soup into serving bowls. Top with edamame, ham and pine nuts to serve.

Gazpacho

Prep Time 5 minutes Cook Time 25 minutes Serves 4

Ingredients:

- 1 red onion, finely chopped
- 3 vine-ripened tomatoes, chopped
- 1 red capsicum, chopped
- 2 celery sticks, chopped
- 425g can diced tomatoes
- 2 1/2 cups (625ml) cold vegetable stock
- 1 tablespoon Worcestershire sauce
- A few drops of Tabasco sauce
- To Serve - Diced feta, chopped parsley
- leaves, pepper and olive oil

Method

1. Place the onion, tomato, capsicum, canned tomatoes, cold stock, celery, Worcestershire sauce, Tabasco and garlic into the Soup Maker Jug. Season with salt.
2. Place the Lid on and select the Smooth setting, then press start.
3. When ready, pour the soup into a jug and chill for 30 minutes.
4. Serve in bowls, topped with feta, parsley and pepper. Drizzle with olive oil to serve.
5.

Curried Pumpkin Soup with Hummus

Prep Time 5 minutes Cook Time 25 minutes Serves 4

Ingredients:

- 600g pumpkin, chopped
- 200g potato, chopped
- 1 leek, white part only, washed and
- sliced
- 2 cloves garlic, crushed
- 3 cups (750ml) hot vegetable stock
- 2 teaspoons mild curry powder
- Pistachio dukkha, hummus, sliced red
- chilli and coriander, to serve

Method

1. Place the pumpkin, potato, leek, celery, garlic, hot stock and curry powder into the Soup Maker Jug.
2. Place the Lid on the Jug and select the Smooth setting. Press start.
3. When the soup is ready, season with salt, place the Lid on and press and hold the Smoothie/Blend Button for 15 seconds before serving.
4. Pour into serving bowls. Top with dukkha, hummus, chilli and coriander to serve.

Mixed Mushroom Soup with Haloumi

Prep Time 5 minutes Cook Time 25 minutes Serves 4

Ingredients:

- 300g button mushrooms, sliced
- 300g Swiss brown mushrooms, sliced
- 200g potato, chopped
- 1 leek, white part only, washed and
- sliced
- 2 cloves garlic, crushed
- 2 1/2 cups (625ml) hot vegetable stock
- 2 tablespoons Worcestershire sauce
- 200g halloumi, sliced
- To Serve - Dried red chilli flakes

- and rosemary

Method

1. Place the mushrooms, potato, leek, garlic, hot stock, and sauce into the Soup Maker Jug.
2. Place the Lid on the Jug, select the Smooth setting, and press start.
3. Season with salt when the soup is ready, place the Lid on the Jug, press, and hold the Smoothie/Blend Button for 15 seconds before serving.
4. Meanwhile, heat a large non-stick frying pan over high heat. Add halloumi; cook for 2 minutes on each side or browned and hot. Cut in half.
5. Pour into serving bowls. Top with halloumi, chilli flakes and rosemary to serve.

Sweet Potato and Red Lentil Soup

Prep Time 5 minutes Cook Time 25 minutes Serves 4

Ingredients:

- 600g orange sweet potato, chopped
- 100g potato, chopped
- 1/2 cup dried red lentils, cooked
- 1 brown onion, finely chopped
- 2 cloves garlic, crushed
- 2 1/2 cups (625ml) hot vegetable stock
- ¾ cup (180ml) coconut cream
- 2 teaspoons ground cumin
- To Serve - Coriander sprigs and black
- sesame seeds

Method

1. Place the potatoes, lentils, onion, garlic, hot stock and cumin into the Soup Maker Jug.
2. Place the Lid on and select the Smooth setting, then press start.
3. Season with salt and add the coconut cream when the soup is ready. Place the Lid on and press and hold the Smoothie/Blend Button for 15 seconds before serving.
4. Pour soup into serving bowls. Top with coriander and black sesame seeds to serve.

Pea and Broad Bean Soup with Prosciutto

Prep Time 5 minutes Cook Time 25 minutes Serves 4

Ingredients:

- 500g frozen peas, thawed
- 200g frozen broad beans, thawed, peeled
- 150g potato, chopped
- 1 brown onion, finely chopped
- 2 cloves garlic, crushed
- 3 1/3 cups (780ml) hot vegetable stock
- 1/3 cup pure cream
- 3 thin slices prosciutto

- To Serve - Chopped chives and
- sour cream

Method

1. Place the peas, beans, potato, onion, garlic and hot stock into the Soup Maker Jug.
2. Place the Lid on and select the Smooth setting, then press start.
3. When the soup is ready, season with salt, add the cream, place the Lid on the Jug, press, and hold the Smoothie/Blend Button for 15 seconds before serving.
4. Meanwhile, heat a large non-stick frying pan over high heat. Add prosciutto and cook for 1 minute on each side or until browned and crispy.
5. Roughly chop.
6. Pour soup into serving bowls. Top with sour cream, prosciutto, and chives to serve.

Roast Tomato and Basil Soup

Prep time: 10 minutes Cook time: 40 minutes Serves: 4

Ingredients:

- 8 very ripe tomatoes cut in half
- 2 red onions cut into wedges
- 4 garlic cloves
- 1 tbsp olive oil
- 1 tbsp balsamic vinegar
- Salt and ground black pepper
- 750ml chicken stock, made from stock cubes
- 2 tsp tomato puree
- 1 tsp brown sugar
- 10g fresh basil

Method

1. Preheat the oven to 200oC / Gas Mark 6.
2. Place the tomato's skin side up into a roasting tin with the red onion and garlic. Drizzle over the olive oil balsamic vinegar and season with salt and milled pepper. Roast for 20 minutes until softened and slightly charred.
3. Carefully place the roasted vegetables into the Soup Maker, pour in the chicken stock, add the tomato puree, brown sugar, fresh basil.
4. Select the smooth setting. Once the soup is ready, season to taste and serve.

Butternut Squash, Chilli and Coconut Soup

Prep time 15 minutes Cook time 30 minutes Serves 4

Ingredients:

- 2 tbsp olive oil
- 500g butternut squash, deseeded, peeled and cut into small cubes
- 1 tsp ground cumin
- 1 large red chilli, finely chopped (remove the seeds for a milder taste)
- 3 garlic cloves, sliced
- 1 medium onion, chopped
- 1 tsp fresh ginger
- 500ml vegetable stock, made from cube
- 200ml coconut milk
- Juice of 1 lime
- 10g fresh coriander

Method

1. In a large frying pan, heat the olive oil and fry the butternut squash for 2-3 minutes, stirring every so often.
2. Add the ground cumin, chilli, garlic, and onion; continue to cook for a further 5 minutes until the ingredients start to soften.
3. Transfer to the Soup Maker and add the remaining ingredients; mix ingredients with a spoon or spatula to evenly distribute.
4. Place the Lid on the Jug and select the chunky setting.
5. Once ready, season to taste and serve. If you want a smooth soup, simply press the blend button until you have your desired consistency.

Quick and Easy Pea, Ham, and Mint Soup

Prep time 5 minutes Cook time 21 minutes Serves 4

Ingredients:

- 600g frozen peas
- 20g fresh mint, leaves only
- 225g quality cooked ham, chopped/shredded
- 100g potato, diced
- 800ml hot stock, from cube (ham)
- Salt and ground black pepper
- 2tbsp olive oil
- 75ml (3 heaped tbsp) crème fraiche

Method

1. Place the peas, mint, ham, and hot stock into the soup maker and select the smooth setting.

2. Season with a bit of salt and milled pepper, add the olive oil and crème Fraiche and using the blend button, blend the soup again for 20 seconds and serve.

French Style Pistou

Prep time 15 minutes Cook time 30 minutes Serves 4

Ingredients:

- 1 courgette (150g), finely diced
- 1 small potato (70g), finely diced
- 1 small onion (70g), finely diced
- 1 carrot (50g), finely diced
- 1 tin of chopped tomatoes (400g)
- 50g petit pois
- 50g spaghetti, broken into pieces
- 50g French beans, cut into 1cm pieces
- 650ml of vegetable stock, from cube
- 1 tbsp tomato puree (mix into the store)

To Serve:

- Pesto
- Parmesan cheese

Method

1. Place the soup ingredients into the Soup Maker. Season with salt and milled pepper and stir with a spoon or spatula.
2. Select the chunky setting and simply wait for the Soup Maker to finish.
3. Serve straight away with a spoonful of pesto and freshly grated parmesan cheese.

Chinese Style Chicken and Sweetcorn Soup.

Prep time: 20 minutes Cook time: 30 minutes Serves: 4

Ingredients:

- 100g sweetcorn, from the cob or tinned, drained
- 1 red onion, finely chopped
- 100g mushrooms, thinly sliced
- 1 tsp fresh ginger, grated
- 50g cooked chicken, shredded
- 1 garlic clove, crushed
- 1.2L chicken stock
- 2tsp cornflour mixed with 1 tsp of water to form a paste
- 2tsp soy sauce
- 50-100g hot cooked noodles
- 1 red chilli, deseeded and finely chopped
- 15g spring onions, finely chopped
- 10g chopped coriander

Method

1. Place the sweetcorn kernels into the Soup Maker and the mushrooms, red onion, ginger, shredded chicken garlic, stock, and soy sauce. Pour in the cornflour paste and stir with a spoon or spatula.
2. Select the chunky setting and leave until ready.
3. Divide the hot cooked noodles between serving bowls scatter over the chilli, spring onions, and coriander. Pour the soup over the noodles and serve.

Chicken and Mushroom Soup

Prep time: 20 minutes Cook time: 30 minutes Serves: 4

Ingredients:

- 2 tbsp olive oil
- 1 medium onion, finely chopped
- 1 garlic clove, chopped
- 240g mushrooms, thinly sliced

- 100g cooked chicken, shredded
- 10g parsley, chopped
- 1 medium potato, finely cubed
- 1litre chicken stock, fresh or made from cube
- 100ml whipping cream

Method

1. Add the olive oil to a large frying pan and fry the onion until soft but not browned.
2. Add the garlic and mushrooms and continue to cook until the mushrooms have softened.
3. Transfer to the Soup Maker with the shredded chicken, parsley, potato, and stock. Select the smooth setting and simply wait for 21 minutes until the soup maker has finished.
4. Season with salt and milled pepper and serve with a drizzle of cream.

Winter Lamb and Lentil Broth

Prep time 15 minutes Cook time 30 minutes Serves 4

Ingredients:

- 2 tbsp olive oil
- 75g lamb mince
- 1 medium onion (100g), finely chopped
- 2 garlic cloves, chopped
- 1 small carrot (50g), finely chopped
- 1 potato (100g), finely chopped
- 1 medium turnip (100g), finely chopped
- 1 tbsp plain flour
- 900ml lamb stock, made from 2 cubes
- 1 tin (400g) of cooked lentils, drained
- ½ tsp chopped rosemary
- 2 bay leaves
- 1tsp Worcestershire sauce

- 1tbsp chopped parsley

Method

1. In a large frying pan, heat the olive oil and fry the lamb, onion, garlic, carrot, potato, and turnip until the lamb has sealed and starts to brown.
2. Stir in the plain flour, then add half of the lamb stock and remove from the heat.
3. Pour the lamb into the Soup Maker with the remaining stock and the last of the ingredients. Season with a bit of salt and milled pepper, mix ingredients with a spoon or spatula to evenly distribute, select the chunky setting and leave until ready.

Cauliflower Velouté with Chorizo Oil

Prep Time 5 minutes Cook Time 25 minutes Serves 4

Ingredients

For the soup:

- 1 head of cauliflower, leaves removed, and cauliflower chopped as small as possible (can use a food processor if necessary)
- 50g unsalted butter
- 1 large onion, peeled and thinly sliced
- 800ml chicken stock
- 1 sprig rosemary
- 50ml double cream
- Good quality sea salt
- Black pepper

For the chorizo oil:

- 100g soft cooking chorizo
- Olive oil

Method

For the soup:

1. Put the butter in the Jug and press the sauté button. Add a little dash of oil to ensure the butter does not burn.
2. After 1 minute, add the sliced onions and rosemary, and cook until soft and slightly browned, using a spatula or wooden spoon to keep the onion mix moving.
3. Add the chopped cauliflower and stir the mixture using the spatula.
4. Add the chicken stock, allow the liquid to a gentle simmer, and add the cream.
5. Place the Lid on the Jug, and select the 'smooth' setting (for the automated time of 21 minutes) when the soup is ready, season with sea salt and black pepper.

For the chorizo oil:

1. Chop the chorizo into 2cm size pieces and place into an ovenproof dish, adding a glug of olive oil.
2. Place the dish into an oven, preheated to 200°C, and roast for 15 to 20 minutes.
3. Remove from the oven. Place a sieve over a bowl, and pour in the chorizo and oil – you'll get a beautiful red oil in the bowl.
4. Serve the soup in warm bowls, and drizzle the chorizo oil liberally over the top. Serve with crusty white bread.

Roasted Carrot and Coriander Soup

Prep Time 15 minutes Cook Time 25 minutes Serves 4

Ingredients

- 500g carrots, peeled and chopped
- Olive oil
- 1 tsp honey
- 2 shallots, peeled and chopped

- 50g unsalted butter
- 1 garlic clove, crushed
- 1 pinch of ground coriander
- 800ml chicken stock (vegetable stock will work just as well)
- 1 large bunch of coriander, leaves removed and set to one side, and stalks finely chopped
- 2 tbsp Greek yogurt
- sea salt
- Black pepper

Method

1. Preheat an oven to 185°C.
2. Place the chopped carrots into a baking tray, coat in the olive oil and honey, and roast in the oven for 25 minutes until they become soft and caramelized.
3. Remove and set aside.
4. Add the butter to the Jug and press the sauté button.
5. Add a splash of oil to ensure the butter does not burn, and once the butter has melted and started to bubble, add the chopped shallots and crushed garlic and allow to cook for 2 minutes until soft.
6. Add the ground coriander and cook for a further minute, then turn off the sauté function.
7. Carefully add the roasted carrots and chopped coriander stalks into the Jug and stir to incorporate.
8. Add the stock, place the Lid onto the Jug and select the smooth setting (for the automated time of 21 minutes).
9. Season to taste with sea salt and black pepper when the soup is ready. Serve in warm bowls with a dollop of yogurt and some freshly chopped coriander.

French Onion Soup with a Gruyère Crouton

Prep Time 5 minutes Cook Time 25 minutes Serves 4

Ingredients

- 500g white onion, sliced
- 5 tbsp of olive oil
- 6 sprigs of thyme

- sea salt
- 1 tsp soft brown sugar
- 1 garlic clove, peeled and crushed
- 125ml white wine
- 750ml beef stock
- 6 slices of baguette
- 125g of grated Gruyère
- Cheese

Method

1. Add the oil to the Jug and press the sauté button.
2. After 1 minute, add the sliced onions, olive oil, and thyme sprigs.
3. Season with salt and stir to combine using the spatula – keep the sliced onions moving in the Jug until they become soft and slightly browned. This will take around 10 to 12 minutes.
4. Add the crushed garlic and stir.
5. Still using the sauté setting, add the wine and bubble and cook off the alcohol.
6. Add the beef stock and turn off the sauté setting.
7. Place the Lid onto the Jug and select the chunky setting (for the automated time of 28 minutes).
8. Meanwhile, in a preheated oven, toast the baguette slices on a baking tray for 10 minutes, turning them over halfway through.
9. When the alarm sounds and the soup is made, ladle the soup into heatproof bowls and top with the two slices of toasted baguette.
10. Sprinkle the grated Gruyère over the top and place it under a hot grill until the cheese is bubbling.

Cream of Tomato Soup

Prep Time 5 minutes Cook Time 25 minutes Serves 4

Ingredients

For the toastie:

- 100g mature Cheddar, grated
- 1 jar of onion chutney (330g)

- 4 slices of brioche

For the soup:

- 1 carrot
- 1 stick of celery
- 1 medium onion
- 1 garlic clove
- Olive oil
- 2 vegetable stock cubes
- 1 400g tin plum tomatoes
- 3 large ripe tomatoes, chopped
- 1 handful of fresh basil
- 50ml double cream
- 1 liter of boiling water
- sea salt
- Black pepper

Method

For the toastie:

1. Spread the onion chutney onto one side of the brioche, add the grated Cheddar, and top with the other slice.
2. Place the sarnie into a dry pan and toast on medium heat until golden brown; this should take around 1 minute (take care as it can burn quickly if left unattended).
3. Flip the sarnie over and toast the other side for a further minute, then remove from the heat and set aside while you prepare the soup.

For the soup:

1. Prepare your ingredients: peel and slice the carrots, slice the celery, peel and chop the onions, and peel and finely chop the garlic.
2. Add a glug of oil to the Jug and press the sauté button.
3. Add all the chopped ingredients and sauté for 8 to 10 minutes, stirring with the spatula until soft.
4. Turn off the sauté setting, crumble in the two stock cubes and add 1 liter of boiling water.

5. Add the tinned and freshly chopped tomatoes and the stalks from the basil, and pour in the cream. Pop the Lid onto the Jug and select the smooth setting.
6. When the alarm goes after the automated time of 21 minutes, the soup is ready—season with salt and black pepper.
7. Preheat the oven to 180°C and put the grilled cheese sarnies into cook for 4 to 5 minutes. Serve on the side of the soup.

Gazpacho with Rosemary Oil

Prep Time 5 minutes Cook Time 25 minutes Serves 4

Ingredients

For the soup:

- 2 slices of crusty sourdough bread, ripped into chunks
- 500g plum tomatoes, cut into quarters
- 1 red onion, peeled and chopped
- 2 garlic cloves, crushed
- 1 small bunch of basil
- 1 red chilli, split lengthways down the center (if you're not a fan of heat, remove the seeds)
- 100ml tomato passata
- 50ml extra virgin olive oil
- 3 tbsp good quality sherry vinegar
- 1 tsp of quality sea salt
- Black pepper

For the rosemary oil:

- 100ml olive oil
- 3 stalks of rosemary

Method

1. Put the tomatoes, onion, garlic, basil, bread, chilli, and passata into a mixing bowl and mix well.
2. Add the sherry vinegar, olive oil, and salt. Cover and pop into the fridge overnight if made in advance.
3. Put the olive oil and rosemary in a pan and place on low heat for 5 minutes to infuse the flavour.
4. Place all the marinated ingredients into the Jug, select the smoothie/blend setting, put on the Lid, and press the start/stop button. Allow to blitz for 4 to 5 minutes until it reaches a smooth, soupy consistency.
5. Carefully remove the Lid, check the seasoning, and serve in chilled bowls with a drizzle of rosemary oil and a sprinkle of sea salt flakes.

Hot & Sour Soup

Prep Time 5 minutes Cook Time 25 minutes Serves 4

Ingredients

- 1 garlic clove
- 1 fresh red chilli
- Good quality sea salt
- 1 thumb-sized piece of ginger
- 100g shiitake mushrooms, sliced
- 100g bamboo shoots, drained
- Groundnut oil
- 4 tbsp soy sauce
- 5 tbsp rice wine vinegar
- 1 teaspoon acacia honey
- 1 liter of hot vegetable stock
- 60g tofu, diced
- 2 spring onions
- Bunch of chives, finely chopped
- 1 large free-range egg
- Black pepper

Method

1. Peel the garlic and deseed the chilies, then roughly chop and place into a pestle and mortar. Bash to a rough paste.
2. Peel and finely chop the ginger and add to the pestle and mortar, then bash until incorporated (if you don't have a pestle and mortar, use a food processor). This can be done by hand, using a sharp knife, if you do not have the equipment.
3. Add a glug of oil to the Jug and select the sauté setting.
4. After a minute, add the mushrooms and bamboo shoots, and fry until golden.
5. Stir in the smashed chilli paste using the spatula and fry for a further minute.
6. Mix 3 tablespoons of soy sauce, 4 tablespoons of rice wine vinegar, honey, and a crack of black pepper. Stir the mixture into the Jug and cook for a minute.
7. Pour in the stock and bring to a simmer.
8. Season with soy sauce and vinegar, place the Lid onto the Jug, and select the smooth setting (for the automated time of 21 minutes). When the alarm sounds, carefully remove the Lid and set it aside.
9. Chop the tofu into small cubes, finely slice the spring onions and whisk the egg.
10. Slowly add the beaten egg to the soup mixture, stirring the soup continuously to form thin egg ribbons.
11. Add in the tofu and leave for 2 to 3 minutes to warm through.
12. Using a spoon, serve in warm bowls with the spring onions and chives scattered on top.

Pea & Coconut Soup

Prep Time 5 minutes Cook Time 25 minutes Serves 4

Ingredients

- 10ml olive oil
- 500g frozen peas
- 2 banana shallots, peeled & chopped (small white onions will also work)
- 2 cloves of garlic, finely chopped
- 400ml whole fat coconut milk
- 800ml vegetable stock (dilute two veg stock cubes in hot water)
- 1 small handful of fresh mint
- leaves, roughly chopped

- 1 sourdough loaf
- Good quality sea salt
- Black pepper

Method

1. Add the oil to the Jug and press the sauté button.
2. After 1 minute, add the chopped shallots and garlic, and use the spatula to keep the ingredients moving for 4 to 5 minutes until the shallots become soft and slightly browned.
3. Add the peas and stir using the spatula. Then add the stock and coconut milk, and turn off the sauté function.
4. Pop the Lid onto the Jug and select the smooth setting (using the automated time of 21 minutes).
5. When the timer goes off, carefully remove the Lid, check the seasoning, and serve in warm bowls, garnishing with roughly chopped mint leaves.

Roasted Jerusalem Artichoke Soup

Prep Time 5 minutes Cook Time 25 minutes Serves 4

Ingredients

- 400g Jerusalem artichokes, peeled and chopped
- 50g unsalted butter
- 1 large onion, peeled and thinly sliced
- 800ml chicken stock
- Olive oil
- 1 sprig thyme
- 50ml double cream
- Truffle oil
- Good quality sea salt
- Black pepper

Method

1. Put the butter in the Jug and press the sauté button.
2. Add a dash of olive oil to ensure the butter does not burn.

3. After 1 minute, add the sliced onions and thyme, and cook until soft and slightly browned, using a spatula or wooden spoon to stir.
4. Add the chopped artichokes and stir through the mixture.
5. Turn off the sauté setting and add the chicken stock and cream.
6. Place the Lid on the Jug and select the smooth setting (for the automated time of 21 minutes).
7. When the alarm sounds, the soup is ready. Season with sea salt and black pepper, and add a good glug of truffle oil. Serve in warm bowls – and if you're feeling fancy, add a swirl of truffle oil when serving.

Mulligatawny Soup

Prep Time 5 minutes Cook Time 25 minutes Serves 4

Ingredients

- 1 onion, chopped
- 2 cloves garlic, crushed
- 1 red chilli, chopped
- 1 tbsp curry powder
- 100g red lentils, rinsed
- 2 celery sticks, chopped
- 1 carrot (approx 100g), chopped
- 1 potato (approx 150g), chopped
- 1 apple, peeled and chopped
- 1 vegetable stock pot/cube
- Fresh coriander to garnish
- Salt and pepper to taste

Method

1. Optionally saute the onion and garlic.
2. Add all the remaining ingredients to the soup maker.
3. Add water (I use hot water) up to the MAX line in the soup maker. Stir all the ingredients together until they are well mixed.
4. Set the soup maker off on chunky.

5. At the end of the soup maker cycle, you can do a quick partial blend or pulse to alter the consistency or leave it as it is.
6. Season according to taste.

POTATO JALAPENO SOUP MAKER

Prep Time 5 minutes Cook Time 25 minutes Serves 4

This unusual combination makes for a subtly spicy soup that is delightful. The coalescence of the mildness from potatoes and the heat from jalapeno peppers will make your taste buds sing. Comprising of vegetables only, this is also a vegan-friendly recipe.

Ingredients

- 2 tbsp vegetable oil
- 2 medium onions
- 2 cloves garlic
- 3 cups vegetable stock
- 4 large potatoes
- 2 jalapeno peppers
- ¼ cup cream
- ½ cup shredded cheddar cheese
- 2 tsp salt
- 1 tsp lemon pepper powder
- 1 tsp turmeric powder
- 1 tsp cumin powder
- 1 tsp dried chives

Method

1. Prepare the vegetables; peel and chop the onions and garlic into small cubes. Peel the potatoes and roughly dice them into little chunks. Handle the jalapeno peppers with caution as their heat causes a burning sensation upon contact with bare skin. It is best to wear disposable gloves before cutting into them. Cut the jalapeno peppers in half and deseed them by scooping out the seeds with the help of a spoon and then finely dice them.

2. In a large pot over medium-high heat, add oil and wait until it is heated sufficiently. Once it reaches that stage, add in chopped onions and garlic. Stir and cook them for a couple of minutes until they become fragrant and translucent. Following this, add in the chopped jalapeno peppers and diced potatoes. Let them meld together for five minutes before adding the spices and condiments.
3. Sprinkle in one by one salt, lemon pepper, turmeric, and cumin powder along with dried chives and stir together to combine. Following this, add vegetable stock and cream and stir to combine. After this, close the Lid and let the soup simmer on medium-high heat for thirty minutes until the potatoes become soft.
4. Once the potatoes are cooked through, turn off the heat and use an immersion blender to transform it into a smooth and creamy mixture. While the soup is still hot, mix in the shredded cheese. Before serving, you can garnish it with a sprinkling of chives and sliced jalapenos for added zing.

Tomato & Basil Soup

Prep Time 5 minutes Cook Time 20 minutes Serves 4

Ingredients

- 3 shallots, chopped
- 4 cloves garlic, crushed
- 5 medium tomatoes, chopped
- 1 medium potato, chopped
- 1 large carrot, peeled and chopped
- 8 basil leaves, chopped
- 800 ml vegetable stock
- 2 basil leaves, chopped, for garnish

Method

1. Add all the ingredients (except the basil) to your soup maker. Stir ingredients together. Make sure you don't go over the MAX line. If you are not above the MIN line, add some more hot water to top it up.
2. Put the Lid on and select the smooth setting.
3. Once the program has finished, take the Lid off and add the chopped basil leaves. Blend on the manual setting for about 20 seconds.

4. Garnish with some chopped basil.

Amount Per Serving: CALORIES: 90

Pumpkin soup

Prep Time 5 minutes Cook Time 20 minutes Serves 4

Ingredients

- 375 g pumpkin
- 1 clove of garlic
- 1.5 sweet potato
- dash of olive oil
- ginger (2 cm x 2 cm)
- chili pepper as desired
- 1.5 Tbsp vegetable broth
- 750 ml water

Method

1. Chop the vegetables into bite-sized pieces and place them in the soup maker.
2. Add the curry paste, stock, and water.
3. Select the 'Smooth' program.
4. Enjoy!

Curry soup with pumpkin and parsnip

INGREDIENTS

- 190 g carrots
- 190 g parsnip
- 225 g pumpkin
- 1.5 tsp Thai red curry paste
- 1.5 tbsp vegetable broth
- 900 ml water

- coconut milk to taste

Method

1. Chop the vegetables into bite-sized pieces and place them in the soup maker.
2. Add the curry paste, stock and water, and coconut milk to taste.
3. Select the 'Smooth' program.
4. Enjoy!

TOMATO-CARROT SOUP

Ingredients

- 1 clove of garlic
- 2 stalks of celery
- 600 g tomatoes
- 200 g carrots
- 1.5 Tbsp vegetable broth
- 750 ml water

Method

1. Chop the vegetables into bite-sized pieces and place them in the soup maker.
2. Add the curry paste, stock, and water.
3. Select the 'Smooth' program.
4. Enjoy!

PEA SOUP

Ingredients

- 1 white of leek
- 600 g peas
- 2 tbsp vegetable broth
- 900 ml water
- dash of olive oil
- a few sprigs of mint
- seasoning salt

Method

1. Chop the leek into bite-sized pieces and place them in the soup maker with the peas.
2. Add the olive oil, stock, and water.
3. Select the 'Smooth' program.
4. Mix a few sprigs of fresh mint into the fresh soup using the 'blend' function.
5. Serve with seasoning salt.
6. Enjoy!

LETTUCE SOUP

Ingredients

- 400 g lettuce
- 2 shallots
- 2 tbsp olive oil
- 1,5 l vegetable stock

Garnish:

- 100 g cooked quinoa
- juice of 1/2 lemon
- 100 g smoked salmon
- 2 tbsp coarsely chopped chives
- salt and pepper

Method

1. Peel and finely chop the shallots. Wash the lettuce and place all the ingredients in the soup maker.
2. Select the 'Extra smooth' program.
3. Finish the soup with the cooked quinoa, lemon juice, salt, and pepper.
4. Add equal amounts of the chopped smoked salmon to the soup bowls and pour over the soup. Garnish with chives.
5. Enjoy!

SWEET POTATO-PEPPER SOUP

Ingredients

- 2 red onions
- 2 garlic cloves

- 600 g sweet potato
- 2 sweet pointed peppers
- 2 cm ginger
- 250 ml coconut milk
- 700 ml water
- 1 vegetable stock cube
- feta cheese
- salt and pepper

Method

1. Clean the onion, garlic, ginger, and pointed peppers and cut them into chunks. Clean and peel the sweet potatoes and cut them into pieces.
2. Place all ingredients in the soup maker, add the water and coconut milk and finally add the vegetable stock cube.
3. Select the 'Smooth' program.
4. Season to taste with salt and pepper. Crumble the feta cheese.
5. Ladle the soup into bowls and add the feta cheese.
6. Enjoy!

THOM KA KAI SOUP

Prep Time 5 minutes Cook Time 20 minutes Serves 4

Ingredients

- 500 ml chicken stock
- 400 ml coconut cream
- 5 cm ginger
- 4 lime leaves
- 1 stem lemongrass
- red chili pepper
- 200 g shiitake
- 2,5 tbsp fish sauce
- 200 g chicken fillet
- 200 g pink prawns
- coriander
- 1 tbsp sugar
- 3 spring onions
- 2 tbsp lime juice
- 3 garlic cloves

Method

1. Clean and finely chop the spring onions, red pepper, ginger, lemongrass, and garlic.
2. Slice the shiitake and cut the chicken fillet into strips.

3. Place the spring onions, red pepper, ginger, lemongrass, garlic, shiitake, chicken, and pink shrimps in the soup maker, add the stock and coconut milk, and finally add the fish sauce and sugar.
4. Select the 'Chunky' program.
5. Flavor the soup with fresh coriander and lime juice.
6. Enjoy!

Beetroot soup with healthy cream

Prep Time 5 minutes Cook Time 20 minutes Serves 4

Ingredients

- 2 beetroot
- 2 carrots
- 1 parsnip
- 1 onion
- 2 garlic cloves
- a splash of olive oil
- 1,5 l vegetable stock
- a few sprigs of lemon thyme

- healthy cream:
- 100 g cashews
- 1 garlic clove
- 0,5 lime juice
- 150 ml water
- 0,25 tsp turmeric
- 0,25 tsp cumin
- a pinch of salt

Method

1. Peel the beetroot, carrots, and parsnip. Peel the onion and garlic cloves. Cut all vegetables into chunks and place them in the soup maker. Select the 'Smooth' program.
2. Place all the ingredients for the healthy cream in a blender and mix until smooth.
3. Spoon the smooth soup into bowls. Garnish with a spoonful of the healthy cream and a sprig of lemon thyme.
4. Enjoy!

Mixed vegetable soup for all seasons

Prep Time 10 minutes Cook Time 20 minutes Serves 4

Ingredients

- 250 gms mixed vegetables I have used a mix of carrots, beans, green peas, and cauliflower
- 120 gms potatoes
- 1 1/2 tbsp chopped garlic
- 1 cup chicken stock or vegetable stock
- 1 cup coconut milk
- 1 tbsp curry powder alternately, you can use Maggi masala
- salt and pepper as required
- 2 tbsp chopped spring onion for garnish
- 2 tbsp coconut cream for garnish

Method

1. Chop all the vegetables into small cubes.
2. Put all the ingredients, except for garnish, into the soup maker.
3. Fill it up with water up to the minimum mark.
4. Stir it all around and close the Lid.
5. Plugin the soup maker and bring the mode to 'pureed soap indicator. Switch it on.
6. In 20 minutes, your soup is ready. Wait for a couple of minutes before opening the Lid. Keep your face away from the Lid while opening.
7. Pour the soup in bowls or mugs and garnish with chopped spring onions, pepper, and some coconut cream. Serve with some croutons or breadsticks.

Tomato-Red Bell Soup

Prep Time 5 minutes Cook Time 20 minutes Serves 4

Ingredients

- 5 tomatoes medium
- 1/2 red bell pepper large
- 3 cloves garlic fat, peeled
- 1 onion medium, peeled
- 600 ml vegetable stock water stock unsalted or use + cube
- 1 tsp salt
- 2 tsp oat flour water + 3 tbsps
- Basil leaves
- Mustard flowers
- Cream Single

Method

1. Quarter the tomatoes. Chop the bell pepper into 2 cm squares (small dice). Slice the onions and finely chop the garlic.
2. Add all of this along with the stock into the soup maker. Close the Lid properly.
3. Switch on the power and select the first function (creamy soup). Press the start button.
4. This will take 25 minutes in all.
5. Once it's done, add the salt, oat flour + water slurry, and close the soupmaker; select the 'Chunky soup' option. In two minutes, this would have come to a boil; at this point, use the Manual Blender option to ensure the oats have mixed into the smooth to give a creamy texture.
6. Pour into bowls, garnish and serve with your favorite bread rolls.

ONE LAST THING...

If you enjoyed this book or found it useful, I'd be very grateful if you'd post a short review on Amazon. Your support really does make a difference and I read all the reviews personally so I can get your feedback and make this book even better.

Thanks again for your support!

Printed in Great Britain
by Amazon